To Ian and Marion
from
Bill & Carol
Barker
For 'Auld Lang Syne'

# Shaped by Vision

## A Biography of
## Theodore Austin-Sparks
1888 – 1971



by
Rex G. Beck